The Ship

JOHN HARTLEY WILLIAMS grew up in London and has worked in France, the former Yugoslavia and Francophone Africa. Since 1976 he has lived in Berlin.

He has published nine collections of poetry, two of which were shortlisted for the T.S. Eliot Prize. The latest collection shortlisted for this award was *Blues* (Jonathan Cape, 2004). He has published translations from German, French, Serbo-Croatian as well as versions of the Rumanian poet Marin Sorescu: *Censored Poems* (2001) Bloodaxe. He has published reviews and essays widely in UK poetry magazines and literary journals.

He has also written a prose memoir *Ignoble Sentiments* (1995), published by Arc, and a mysterious prose work called *Mystery in Spiderville*, reissued in paperback by Vintage (2003). A reader-friendly guide to the writing of poetry called *Teach Yourself Writing Poetry*, co-written with the Irish poet Matthew Sweeney, was reissued in a revised edition by Hodder in 2004. A privately printed book of poems and photographs *North Sea Improvisation* (2003), set in and around Cuxhaven on the North Sea German coast, is available from the poet.

Also by John Hartley Williams

POETRY
- *Blues* (2004)
- *North Sea Improvisation: a Fotopoem* (2003)
- *Mystery in Spiderville* prose poems (2003)
- *Spending Time with Walter* (2001)
- *Canada* (1997)
- *Double* (1994)
- *Cornerless People* (1990)
- *Bright River Yonder* (1987)
- *Hidden Identities* (1982)

MEMOIR
- *Ignoble Sentiments* (1995)

NON-FICTION
- *Teach Yourself Poetry* with Matthew Sweeney (2004)

TRANSLATION
- *Censored Poems* translations of Marin Sorescu (2001)

The Ship

John Hartley Williams

SALT

CAMBRIDGE

PUBLISHED BY SALT PUBLISHING
PO Box 937, Great Wilbraham, Cambridge CB21 5JX United Kingdom

All rights reserved

© John Hartley Williams, 2007

The right of John Hartley Williams to be identified as the
author of this work has been asserted by him in accordance
with Section 77 of the Copyright, Designs and Patents Act 1988.

This book is in copyright. Subject to statutory exception
and to provisions of relevant collective licensing agreements,
no reproduction of any part may take place without the written
permission of Salt Publishing.

First published 2007

Printed and bound in the United Kingdom by Biddles Ltd, Kings Lynn, Norfolk

Typeset in Swift 9.5 / 13

*This book is sold subject to the conditions that it shall not,
by way of trade or otherwise, be lent, re-sold, hired out,
or otherwise circulated without the publisher's prior consent
in any form of binding or cover other than that in which
it is published and without a similar condition including this
condition being imposed on the subsequent purchaser.*

ISBN 978 1 84471 339 4 hardback

Salt Publishing Ltd gratefully acknowledges
the financial assistance of Arts Council England

ARTS COUNCIL ENGLAND

1 3 5 7 9 8 6 4 2

Contents

Foreword: A Pastel Shade of Blue   vii

Two Poems	1
Greed for Life	2
A Cool Seduction	3
Swimming at Night	4
The Jewel	6
A Little Greek Myth	8
The Sexual Aquarium	9
Hamlet Unbound	10
Heathrow	13
On the Royal Wedding of Princess Anne: November 14th 1973	14
The Permanent Secretary to the Minister for Home Affairs Offers an Explanation	16
Heroes	18
Summer School 1976	19
The Hang-Out	21
Literature	22
Amelia and Caledon	26
My Way	27
Hedge Poet	29
Cat Up the Tree	31
Summa Cum Laude	36
Lübeck	38
Not a Description	40
The Secret	43
Song of the Grillbar Restaurant	45
Communications	46
Poem	47

Who Invited Carstairs?	48
Long John Silver's Song	54
A Moment of Truth in *Le Bar Du Château*	55
To the God of Creative Writing	56
Money	58
Time and Western Man	62
The Dwarf	63
The Dentist	64
My Friend Moultby	66
Lament for the Subotica-Palić Tramway	68
Ten Poems for Treasure	73
The Ship	94
Flea Market	96
Four Seasons	97
My Father was an Interventionist	105
On First Looking into Gittings' 'Keats'	107
Going Home	108
Two for Nerval	109
Magyarország	111
Ode to Paella	117
Five Anecdotes of the Count	118
Moment Abbey	131
Pan's Joke	132

A Pastel Shade of Blue

Most of these poems, written between 1960 and 1980, have never been published before. I'd complete a poem and then the job of finding a stamp, an envelope, and a friendly address to send it to usually proved too much. I haven't been able to establish the actual date of composition reliably, so they're not arranged in some putative chronological order.

Typing up the handwritten or corrected typescripts of poems gave rise to a few hesitations. What exactly *is* this word? Did I really write *that*? Guesswork was sometimes supplanted by the desire to revise, with concomitant tremors of conscience. What do you do when your younger self was clumsy, awkward or just plain stupid? My attitude to an old poem (which is, of course, a *young* poem) has mostly been, as Oscar Wilde said of ignorance, "touch it and the bloom is gone."

Rimbaud's mocking account of the conflict of desire for sexual and/or literary success in an adolescent breast—*On n'est pas sérieux, quand on a dix-sept ans*—could be a snapshot of me at the age of seventeen. In Rimbaud's poem, a young man forsakes café life to brood over the young woman who has laughed at his poems. But then his poems do their work and she writes him a letter. Straightaway he returns to the life of cafés. "*On n'est pas sérieux* . . . Older, still amorous, still dithyrambic, and across-the-channel," I coined the word *extrilism* to describe my pickle. An *ism* word would be just the job to validate the self-extrication of exile and all inexplicable extrapolations from that experience. Serious laughter, in other words. What other available poetic strategy could there be?

Consider a politician announcing a national tragedy. Gawp at his (it's nearly always a man) inadequately performed scenario of gravitas. The only possible response to the discrepancies between the suit, the clichés, and the disaster is the hilarity of anguish. Laughter reveals the paucity of present day reality, throws ink at the sorrowing imposture of the lyric, and replaces the clichés of shadow-discourse with the names of things as they are: axes, bottles, carpets, doctors, eggs, feet, geckoes, hats, igloos, jam pots, kukudus, lamp posts, mistresses, nappies, octopi, penguins, quicksands, rats, sausages, tubs, underwear, violins, whips, ex-wives, yams and zoot-suits. If the names come at you systematised though the alphabet, so much the better; the alphabet is seriously unserious—a bedlam of displaced vocables. Extrilism lives!

No doubt one reason a poet writes is to be more like himself than he or she at present manages, and to be more like yourself, by a paradox, usually requires camouflage. Also, every poet comes to his or her own understanding of the place of poetry in the world—mine was/is that it must be adversarial. How many aliases would be necessary to conduct a sure-fire campaign? Here, jostling for expression, are a few of them: lovers, dentists, dwarves, aristocrats, civil servants, royalty, and pirates. Almost a big enough crowd for an uprising.

I want to dedicate this book to the memory of Dennis Enright, who published my first book. "We can't call you J.H. Williams," he said, "they'll think you're a Welsh prop forward. Do you want to put the Hartley in?" Gently, he helped me to sacrifice the many poems the exigencies of page length demanded. Up till 1982, the series in which I was first published in book form had had poisonous yellow covers. When the book appeared, Dennis sent me a wryly congratulatory message about the cover: "They've given you a pastel shade of blue." I don't know what he would say, standing up there on Parnassus, of this book—but I do know I would brood long and hard over whatever it was.

JOHN HARTLEY WILLIAMS 2007

Dark shoulders have stirred the lightning
A girl's arms have nested the fire
Not I but the handmaid kindled
    Cantat sic nupta
I have eaten the flame

                        Ezra Pound: Canto XXXIX

Two Poems

(I)

Surely and slowly it goes:
all youth to the marriage table,
all honey to the gods.
And old men tuck into their memories
with beards for napkins and eyes for forks.

(II)

Change here for change here:
the beer here is fair there.
I can travel without fear
to anywhere from anywhere.

From both sides of the flag, both sides
are visible.
Nothing, if you use your eyes, is
divisible.

My inner compass can surpass
any mere direction:
the needle simply breaks the glass
and stands up to attention.

Greed for Life

Greed for life: it makes the soldier curl
damp in the grass with a foreign girl,
keeps our myths up there in heaven,
keeps luck upon the count of seven.

Greed for life: it makes the clerk put down
his pen and stare about him with a frown,
imagining that peaks of great event
will rise from boredom's flat extent.

Greed for life: the lover thinks he knows
the pangs he has are simply those
the sanctions of vicissitude decree—
that pain will surely turn to ecstasy?

Or will those happy, small illusions
fail before the paltry meal of life—
the burned toast of a thousand sins,
the sour milk of rage and strife?

No, no. When hunger mounts again
against the daylight and the rain,
what's failed once, what's failed twice,
will keep the gambler at his dice.

Beneath his breath, there is a word,
unfindable, that exercises power,
does not declare itself, remains unheard,
yet stops the clock, redeems the hour.

Greed for life: it makes the soldier curl
damp in the grass with a foreign girl,
keeps our myths up there in heaven,
keeps luck upon the count of seven.

A Cool Seduction

Lift he gets from looking swift
into a girl's blouse, getting hard
at that impossible gleaming
curve, like a suspended fall, a view;

slipping to backchat while
his cardiac hand arrests
her white, unbreathing knee, thigh,
sorting the flesh from the clothes;

her own cool eye elsewhere. She
no doubt, would not take notice of
Hiroshima, happening, perhaps happening
in the depth of all the people she is,

discarding all she is, at last,
from clothes to skin, unskeined—
one shoulder bone of ivory,
her soft but scornful breath.

"Did they do this to you, and this?"
he asks. She looks with eyes of deep-
ening grey and smiles a faraway reply:
Is this the mad take-over of the world?

Swimming at Night

Lights out, the cars are squatting,
queering up the night with radios,
shifting soundlessly through all the gears
of human flesh. Prejudice is back
and lies and moonlight. Quickly,
I strip, the wind's buff
chastens eerily forgotten forks, my
foolish legs are sharpening up their wits.
I split, racy, to the water's edge,
dangle, wave my arms and shout.
Automobiles go bump without desire.
I, outsider, ape, toss body, all
into the water's gross deliverance
and feel its cumbrous depths, the saline glug
of eyewash in my ears and mouth,
the bloop of nakedness that fills
in every crack with drink. Aswim, I go,
slurp the sea's placenta, feel
with every stroke the turbid beast
that throats me. Night-clouds pale
casually towards the dark.
The busy indolence of life
evaporates. The moon's untethered
globe swims up to take
its silent witless place above, revolving
over me forever over me . . .
The agitated melodies of clifftop dreams
dwindle with the cars, departing—back
to brilliant laughter in the town,
the camaraderie of bars. I've swum out
too far, this distance from
the body's anchor makes
the disconnection scary. But liberty

in darkest places reigns, here beneath
a leering cliff, in the sea's clutch,
where toes no longer touch
the squirming, sandy bottom, where
intimately unconfiding tides
are everything and in between
the sea and sky the land
is just an all-confounding scar . . .

The Jewel

We burgled the cat,
two skin-clad thieves,
       to steal ... well, what?
       two cautious selves ...

We broke in naked,
robbing and lying,
       till your eyes looked
       ah! sleepily into mine.

We said: "It's worthless,
this jewel, this prize,"
       and we laughed, senseless
       amid our desires.

From each other we took
each other! we said: "Steal it!
       It's nothing but bother
       to me guarding it."

And your body grew douce,
your flesh like water,
       wild and loose
       my culprit, my daughter.

Now we have tasted
love's hammer on each,
       lie mortal, arrested,
       caught in the flesh.

After the violence
the silence fills
>   the vault of our presence
>   with brilliant jewels.

We became what we stole,
the glorious swag,
>   *cracked our hearts whole*
>   *put the cat in the bag*

A Little Greek Myth

Brilliant armoured Greeks, you pant
for victories—treacherous epics!—
Odysseys I too,
a little out of puff. I'm too fat.

Penelope sings—the slackening weight
of sensuality   leans
into her breast,   her many-
suitored body dawdling,   but

I travel and forget.   Clamour
spoils Aegean stillnesses,   sailors bawl
our sea-quick comradeship,   the
heart pumps. We sail

and on the rock a naiad sculpts. The sea
has ripened   to a shout.   I gasp
out lives upon her shore,   a catch
of jumping fish   mad for her embrace.

Soldiers, wife, children   I desert
to know the Hydrades—absurd!—
whom flesh and rocks entwine,   the breathless self
and its intolerable amours.

The Sexual Aquarium
(Gare D'Austerlitz)

Great fish slither beneath the water
and the world rots to pieces.
I was standing in the station listening to
loudspeakers, when her sexy fingers

tickled my back. *C'était le coup de foudre!*
A picture of ideological villains we were —
a chap with slick chops, a dolly with
blind, straight, hair, speeding in a

coloured motor-car to egophilia.
Zounds! I sank into your aquarium.
Fish eat each other. I shall eat you.
Listening for the train to *Orléans*,

going via somewhere and somewhere
else, I was standing in all my life,
like a puddle, feeling the roof
weep about me, when two mad fish

addressed me from the bottom of
seriousness. "Do you wish to gape
like an adage upon life? Or will you
take this sexy French chick and

humiliate her?" I loved you like
little bubbles rising in the coloured
fish tank. Trains to stations. Me,
slowly, also, as we all arrive and depart.

Hamlet Unbound

Ladies in the stalls are moved to tea
and tragedy, nibbling at a piece of cake
while Lear storms. "Just one lump, please,
not two," then on to fair Cordelia's demise,
followed by the king . . . "Alas,
I do think Shakespeare was a godless man.
His plays are somehow . . . hopeless.
Life is not *completely* black."
The army knots its thick-roped, nine-tailed way
across the boards. In darkness Hector holds
a lustrous shield aloft that glitters through
the building: only bricks and mortar after all.
"This theatre's *awfully* cold. The people
in the ticket office really quite *abrupt*.
So *many* foreigners, I'm sure
they cannot understand a word." Petruchio
weds Kate, she's tumbled there and then,
kaleidoscopic skirts fly up, her legs
are white and pliant as
complying beauty opens blazing lips to verse.
"She is quite *pretty*, I suppose, though rather thin—
it seems to be the fashion nowadays."
And then comes Falstaff's unpacific troop,
their courage suppurating boils
till with his laggard-loving tongue young Henry
pricks. The boils subside. "It's strange
how Falstaff seems to dominate the play,
he's so unworthy of the Prince. You know,
it's fortunate one doesn't understand
that punning. It's really rather crude.
Oh, this is poor Richard Two, his death
is really quite affecting. Let's hope
the bar has not misplaced our order."
The plays conclude, the painted demons lurch

into the wings, the voices moulder
in the gilded cornices, deposit dust
upon the cherubs' wings, the ladies leave
to feel cartharsis in a homeward taxi—
banish fiction, banish all the world

except... there's Hamlet, lonely on the stage,
his shoulders shrugged with pain to feel
the actor moving in his bones and muscle,
a brash and inconsiderate tenant...
The audience reflects: "He's not been so well done
since Stratford '58." Hamlet shakes his head.
Faced with choices more perplexed than being
either absolute for death or life, his
unrestrained and bitter words invent
soliloquies no audience will hear:
"Ophelia, did she go mad just there?
God knows I can abuse. And those
who sit attentive in the dark and listen...?
Do they catch the whiff, the stink
of Gertrude's loins, greasepaint floating
down into the stalls? Can they hear
the termites ticking in my wooden brain?
My father, penned up in this purgatory,
jailed by spotlight in this scented hall,
his soul condemned to histrionics like myself—
do they suppose his ghost is just a trick?
And when they see me gut Polonius,
his aphorisms drip behind the curtain,
what stain do they think *that* is
spreading slowly out across the stage?"
He stands and paces up and down.
His laughter blasts the sparrows from the eaves.
The theatre crumbles to an iron skeleton,

its gilded roof is opened to the sky
and unrehearsed amidst the desolation
the Hero catches at a frozen voice
and turns sardonically, his ear cupped
to seize a final, petrified request:
If I could have one in the second interval.
Yes, thank you. Only one lump, please.

Heathrow

The jets astride the raindrops
whine decrescendo over tiles.
Glow-worm Baby, home to stardom,
money, fumbles with her seat.

Flashbulbs simmer. In their houses,
deep in consternation, thinkers
worry at the facts and start
from reverie—their trousers round their knees.

The cars wash over Westway, lit
with other purposes, salient
desires. A million televisions puff
'Our Island Story'—darkness falls,

and Glow-worm Baby, making news,
allots the jostling cameras each
an intimacy bright as hell:
So glad to be here! Back in good old history!

On the Royal Wedding of Princess Anne: November 14th 1973

The kingdom of crown and ceremony,
embodied in its magic flesh,
marries here, weeping,
full of religion, the people's fear . . .

We are people or gods. It doesn't
matter. Triumphant, come among you,
raising my hand,
I do not see you. I also fear.

Our kingdom is governed with
game and ritual, complicated strokes.
Now I shall try to smile
at the great growl of your approval.

God and his words utter themselves
reverently between us. My piety
will brook no obstacles. We marry
in sumptuous cloth and stone.

The music we had every reason
to be uplifted by, brilliant hounds
of organ and trumpet, scattering
the abbey darkness into rags!

Wailing joy upon my body,
you felt yourself within me: object
of spiritual bliss. Such games. They
hallow me. Keep me amused.

We are ordinary people.
You should see and touch our ordinariness.
I shall fulfil your famishment.
For you, my hymen will bleed.

But naked you will never see me.
Also you may starve, while I eat.
The courtesy you show me
must always bear your weight of loathing.

Yet now in my wedding hope, I tremble
to see behind your deferential faces
engines you have built
that run without a human intervention,

pistons sliding as
the flywheel turns . . . I hear
the roar of unattended instruments
above the organ's clamour,

the gathering momentum of machines
that drives your watchfulness, follow-
ing each move I make
within this dark, uneasy shed.

The Permanent Secretary to the Minister for Home Affairs Offers an Explanation

This is my office, these
are my papers, this my desk, the chair.
All life goes before me in orderly paragraphs.
This is the satinwood box in which I keep
O anything, and this my ruler,
straight as a leap from heart to throat.
Before the low table, a leather couch.
If someone knocks,
I put benevolence and trust around them.
And photos. My wife glints sideways
out of what she does not understand, or
the children have understood it and paled into
the milk-coloured weal, becoming part of nothing.
Observe mahogany, the plush
carpet, the darkened wainscot. That
is a picture of cursing on the wall. This,
I commissioned. Touch. The beauty of art
is to leave one colder, distant. In the course
of ordinary human flood—I work, merely.
Affairs go plain and level
under my writing hand. This, my cabinet
of drink; and these, state papers.

At meetings I endeavour not to speak
too often but turn my head toward
the source of speech. In the net of government
what worms therein is simply what
has sprung therein. We do not fish.
I hear the word 'leviathan', from time to time,
a denizen of national deeps, perhaps, but
we do not fish. This life
is monsterless, although it pays
sometimes to let one's thought amuse itself

where thought has nested. Too late
my underlings will comprehend when
I am angry; too late my loved ones
when I am pleased. Nothing
I predict will be the slightest help
to anyone.
Events must overcome the common man;
uncommon men must tie the knots of fact
and school the future. This,
my myth, the coat, the coat-stand,
keyhole, key that rages in
the lock, the yellow dado's line
against the wall, that draws
its perfect horizontal round this room
and round again
until it strikes my brow, dead-centre.
Of course there is omission
of the senses' dumb configuration
lest reason fail itself. The knot I tie
is only harmless words, which means
the blindfold prisoner slumped against the post
is just a fiction (as he knew himself)
and words alone, we know,
created him. They equally ensure
his failure will not be recalled.
So let's dissolve that face
before it might suggest
the course of anything might be
a better way, beyond the stars—
some other branch of fate,
that we must seal off. There is, you see,
a great alternative. And I
am it.

Heroes

They drubbed fat women to music,
played the lyre and kissed fat tits.
A scalding sun fell hissing
down between the sea's warm lips.

The sea-wind swollen sail walloped
reddish air of maddened eve.
Standing in the prow, the heroes
made much ado of make-believe.

Stories held them, bearded, filthy,
round the teller's wine-stained teeth.
They listened, terrified, to tales
so tall they dwarfed the tiny fleet.

They woke refreshed from awful dreams,
the night's dismay all gone to shreds
and singing went to silver breakfasts,
feats of arms and sexy beds.

What storytime has now become
is flickering and restless minds.
Heroes only to ourselves, we stare
into an ever-opening light that blinds.

Summer School 1976

Squatting against the bookcase, knees
drawn up to chin, you wondered if
the act of pleasure was not overrated.

Summer days. The streets outside were
freighted with the noise of trucks
en route for channel ports, and we were monks

within a garden, walled, sequestered
in an edifice of sun and silence. But in
the toils of need our summer nights grew fierce.

We ate the food of our community
which did not bind us. From the theatre's steep,
we poised to dive into the speaker's voice.

Too knowledgeable acts. Did we think
by listening hard and taking notes we'd find
solutions and confront them? Deptford beat us.

New Cross rued our souls. Our seedling
city grew from elsewhere, all affections
nipped by frost of the departure date.

Squatting by the bookcase, drinking
something, smiling to yourself, you looked up once,
that certain way. What crossed your mind?

Now I wonder, had we turned our shortlived
colloquy to something else, would we still
be standing there upon the season's hazy ground,

the sky still arching over us, an endless blue?
The summer died to clouds and rain. We took
the mind's things home. Later they meant nothing.

Now I write to hold you in my mind,
to recapitulate your voice, dark and earnest, the view
that life holds summers yet before you.

The Hang-Out

In the *Café Antonio*
the ceiling swarms with municipal cherubs,
peeling angels, bellow-cheeked.
Moodily, the artists imitate
this ripe celestial sprawl:
across the tall-backed velvet couches,
or leaning by a quartz-seamed marble pillar—
the immolation of the rest in somnolence.
Through the mockery of gateau-forks,
sarcastic belching of the coffee jug,
ironic dribble of the fountains,
the artists stare at their reflections
faded in the silver-tarnished mirrors,
watch each others' brittle mouths
that gawp and twist on verities
like fish on hooks. Are these
the keepers of the relics?
Idle they are, unquestionably.
Unproductive, certainly.
What rational man
would argue that we should not
stand them at the wall and shoot them?

Literature

999 monkeys pound 999 typewriters, monitored by Hoggenbacker and Strumpff from a console. Months pass. "Hold on," says Hoggenbacker, "I think we've got something." Monkey 301 writes: *to be or not to be that is the question whether 'tis nobler in the fuck pffwwukkk zzzlukkkkshrwtmph.* "No dice," says Hoggenbacker. "Abort 301." There is a flash. 998 monkeys continue to type.

(1)

The ape writes literature, you say?
How shall we read
indifferent chapters such as these?

Like the world, his plots
leave far too many ends untied;
his characters are done in depth
but seem not fully to be understood . . .

How shall we ever read such scenes?

Read on! The ape narrates
such histories!
An artist! He explores!

Each cave-painted cranium
each scratch-sick armpit
the demagogy of the arse
the sly repositories of each toe's crevice
the cud-warm darkness of the hollowed tooth
the haunted whirlpool of the ear
the magic cretin of the navel
the skulking larder of the fingernail
the bulb of murder in the eye
guffawing fountain of the mouth
fantastic garbage of the brain

the wheezy ululation of the heart
trumpery lungs

and the hard marble of the soul
rolling on the polished floor.

So you may well ask as we all did:
what did he find?
what did he find?

   (II)

He found maniac Captains with luscious ladders
rushing to the windows of Duchesses with demands for love.

He found virtuous people staring through a butcher's window,
admiring the raped girl dangling from a hook.

Lurking behind dark glasses he found the almost inanimate
                       Führer of commerce
coughing up timetables, facts, money, nylons, in
                    their sputum.

He found the proud, leopard-shooting, virgin-undoing,
                    tree-uprooting races
occupying wildernesses with their whisky and distaste
                  for form.

He found trigger-happy soldiers sprawled upon the nursery
                    floor
blowing up wooden trains, shelling doll's houses, executing
                    Rosebud on the patterned rug.

and you may well ask, as we all did:
How does he write it down?
What images does he use?

   (III)

The ape writes love stories, you know.
Anchored by his tail within a baobab,
he scribbles in a notebook. Downwind
of love, he sniffs the glandular air
and fornicates between each paragraph,
sagging somewhat at the knees
as if weighed down by love's incurious body.

In a while, he turns his hand
to symbolism—as he writes
the sky turns dark and swans take off.
He conjures up a smell of apple blood
through shiny, gaping, jet-black nostril holes.
His eyes
pop right and left. He grinds
a massive jaw.

He's into realism now—
having babies, being poor, splitting
up and losing out—
he shifts his hairy bottom on the branch
and spits a nut at other
more unliterary apes.

Heroism, valour, courage . . . ?
Imaginary cutlasses go *swish*
within his brain and puzzled heads
of travellers on an omnibus

fall off their necks and roll along the floor.
In wartime watch his eyeballs roll.
He orders executions, firing squads,
dispatches millions to a certain death,
and out of all these millions finds the time
to show the man whose awful fate
is that he's
caught the clap from Jane.

A furry valediction
is composed for each soul lost,
a tragedy by ape,
a monkey ode,
a simian epitaph.

He grunts within a tree and beats off flies —

anthropomorphic publishers
await.

    (IV)

How can we read such pages
when every turn and twist defines despair?

Apes don't write so well.

How does an ape provide
suffering, struggling, coming through?

Expect by the merest
accident

it's all chaos.

Amelia and Caledon
A version of pastoral.

Our village was mud from house to house.
Only the green and brilliant leaves were not muddy.
The pigs, the people, the chickens, the wheeled traffic—
they were all muddy. Squint between the houses,
what you saw were muddy fields.

In the shit-warm sultriness of the byre,
I spoke to her: *Thou art smiling and obedient,*
I muttered. *It likes me well.* Her forehead rested
against the brindled cow. Her long fingers
pulled at the teats. Her boots were up to here in dung.

The rains came each day. We carried
green and soaking logs into the barn to dry.
Sawdust tickled my nostrils. She turned to me
in gloom, her hair flowing from underneath
a primrose kerchief. She dropped her gaze.

What could be more hot, more useless
than poultry? Tripping over squawks, I pursued her
as she gathered speckled eggs into a basket.
Above the counterpoint of brood and cluck,
I spoke with urgency. Rain fell on the roof.

That Sunday, we walked out, through a bog.
It was April. The sky wore a fierce black eye.
Far off and rumbling, there was thunder.
We slithered to the river, high in spate.
Amelia I said *'tis thee I love.*

She opened her mouth to speak. Lightning
flashed. She stepped into my arms; I clutched a spray
of ash. Her face had looked just once on mine, so pale.
And then she had incinerated. Alone, I sloshed
my heavy-booted way back home.

My Way

I was delighted to be taken out and shot.
It made my day.

The following week I was savagely attacked
by a gang of what would have been
ruffians, but for my welcoming courtesies.
They beat me up and left politely. I was charmed.
On Friday I was exquisitely arrested,
divinely humiliated at my place of work,
forced to acknowledge the theft of a period of time
in numerous small increments of minutes,
seconds even, and all the pretty secretaries wept
and my discomfiture thrilled to the raps
of the judge's hammer.

What a sentence that was! They broke
me down and re-assembled me. Ah!
There was still enough me left to enjoy it!
On my release, there were delicately malicious
blackmailers, parole officers, checkers-up.
To comply with their vicious exhortations
I became a prostitute (male), serial killer,
                            and father of four.
I was an impeccable citizen, a model of
                                    gratuitous evil.
They made me Rotary Swine of the Year.
As a social non-misfit, I made an ambiguous sight.
But crowds gathered when
it was discovered I'd fallen down on the job
so completely the job had fallen down with me
and I lay as if at the bottom of a well
smiling up through the wreckage
at the descending brickbats.

Two men in white coats hauled me up
announcing my secret terror
of committing laudable acts
had rendered me terminally unusable for
the illustration of moral choice.
As the great doors of the asylum
clanged shut, I walked out
into bright, corruptible sunshine.

Now I walk a pollen-scented road,
pulling the sky's body down on my chest,
thrusting my hips at every soft tree,
ravishing weeds at their roots,
seducing bees and humping flowers,
getting deep into the earth's warm bed,
unrestrained, in fact, you want
this all to stop?

Well, give me something
other than these words.

Hedge Poet

I strolled along the highway
with my book of dirty songs.
The clouds were moving safely
in the sky where they belonged.

I saw the hills and farmland,
the pasture-heavy flocks.
The road went this way, that way,
and back around the rocks.

Beneath a hedge a maiden lay,
her boyfriend lay on top.
Her ululations grew in waves—
a tide that wouldn't stop.

And now the bloody universe
was lowering down at me.
Its brows of evil dusk
were knitted up in glee.

Alright, I said, I'd write
some poems filthier than it;
I'd whack it with some verses.
I'd trample it a bit.

Flatten pleasure out, I thought,
till back it sprang in pain.
I'd show them once they've done it, how
it simply starts again.

I'd scare the birds in fields with
my appalling yawps of weird.
A backwards-lovely carolling!
I'd get the cosmos queered!

I strode along the highway,
ignited with my mission
to say it as it should be
and bugger the transmission.

Cat Up the Tree

Most of my colleagues in soul
went to prison at age nine or so,
having been thrashed through childhood,
abandoned on station platforms,
left on hot, deserted streets to chew
back tears, misery, digest
their vile indignation. In jail, love's
grievous harm was done to them by psychopaths;
the judge observed that it would teach them an etc.
What could they do but
dream the girl they planned to marry—
her eyes, her breasts, her plenty cash?
They stumbled back to freedomland,
heard mothers rail at them from chicken-stew,
and fathers bawl at them from pin-stripe suits.
The neighbours flung huge clods of earth
and whistled in their pussy-cats.
The only way to flee from that was
PLAY YOUR FIENDISH MUSIC VERY LOUD . . .

My colleagues in soul
have learned nothing.
Indeed they have learned much
from their refusing to learn.
They have lolled on dirty sheets.
They have stared into water.
They have seen the bars in the water, in the sky.
They have seen the women dress like gaolers.
They grabbed their trousers and ran.

My colleagues in soul
are going down stairs very quickly, nervously,
hoping that nobody sees them.
Or staring aghast at monstrous entertainments.

Or not talking back to their boss.
Or sitting in public lavatories writing poems on toilet paper.
Or they are entering bookshops that are dirty only by virtue of
 dust.
Or they are sitting in run-down establishments,
eating a run-down egg.
Or they are being taken up into sybaritic motor-cars
and whirled through soft lights and fed
soft dinners, to be dropped
at the end of the evening, which it is,
in an alley of dustbins and gregarious tramps.
Painstakingly, they are learning foreign languages
in order to be able to say: "I love you."
Painstakingly, they are counting their money,
then forgetting it when they leave.
Painstakingly, (O with what pains!)
they write their poems. (A sample follows):

> *In a dream I was*
> *stolen from myself. Curious fellows*
> *pardoned me. I gazed into the face*
> *of self-advertisement, and, so moral I was,*
> *I beshat my trousers. The moon raced up,*
> *rockets followed her. I heard the Great Sigh*
> *of my audience realising*
> *I had nothing to say.*

My colleagues in soul
went to the University of Rubbish.
They graduated like ripe apples, falling
from trees into the mossy arms of whores.
They crossed the world,
but the world sent them back.
They dreamed of conversing with famous poets.

They stole milk from doorways in foreign cities,
They chased each other, drunken, down the tramlines.
At smelling of an old, true onion,
they sat in tears, in darkness, early brethren, very ripe
 Franciscans.
They heard the restless bumping of the animals in adjacent
 stalls.
Naïve, they were, and dirty; they kept each other warm like pigs
 within a litter.
They laughed a lot. They laughed some more.
The neighbours sent them notes in rusty cans: "Please
stop the laughter!" They couldn't stop.
Eviction orders came. They kept each other
company for miles up the road and wept
at parting, swigging down the final droplets of the wine,
returned to town, broke out in laughter once again.
God would not approve, to hell with Him.
They packed and left.
In the grand outside they met the following:
thin, mealy-mothered people with seborrhoea,
big, friendly, warm-hearted, knife-you-in-the-back moralists,
Bulgarian lady academic expert sociologists with V.D.,
cautious, reserved, intelligent people who were monuments
 to avarice and pride,
radically intellectual wives who'd cut off your balls
 before they lost a point,
men who knew about the levels of meaning in Donne,
diplomatic representatives who'd been to Oxford and
 Cambridge simultaneously,
women who said: "O.K. but hurry up,"
people who were always in a hurry, but slow,
transvestites who were all or nothing at all,
writers who had published books and thought this was it,

very few who had looked into
the quietly orbiting eye of the nothing cat,
swishing its tail in the nothing tree,
showing its teeth from time to time
and remarking: "Nothing," but cleaning
invisible whiskers with fine and feline invisible paws.

Colleagues of soul I have this
to say to you:
To have risen, unbreakfasted, and walked by the river,
watching how the birds cluster and swoop,
how they fly up and make their intricate patterns
above the leafless trees—
is all this, could it be, an idea?
To have crossed the granite of the city
with an eye open for a cheap pie-shop,
and a nose scenting and questing for coffee smells
(your head bent, your coat thin, the wind cold)—
could that
have anything to do with art?
To have gazed out at the undistinguished sea,
the endless procession of the rollers,
the unassuming dullness of the sky;
to have felt the most precise and articulate passion in your
    breast
sink slowly down—
could this mean, is it possible to think,
one might arrive at a revelation?

We should remake the world,
we, the feeble, we who are content with little.
We should laugh to each other across continents,
take each other soup across the language barrier.
In culture nothing is right—
but if you lie back, naked, over the pillows,

she will undress for you if
you desire hard enough and concentrate aptly.
Colleagues of soul,
the cat is up the tree again.
She'd like to have us read to her.
She'd like to read our poems.
But O that pink yawn, those clean paws!
O that promise of the disappearing trick!
Colleagues of soul, in our misuse
is the final understanding of use.

Let's face it:
most foregather where
a tree spreads empty, leafless boughs
upon the air.

Summa Cum Laude

This is the grammar school
where, in the darkness of the vestibule,
a stag dies with perfect authority,

and next to it, on wooden scrolls,
the gilded former pupils glow, who died
that they might be ignored.

"Ah, boys, will you remember
'Jenny' Wrenn? Keeper of clouted backs
and smarting souls?" He smiled. "Be-

fore your drolleries begin, let me
remind you no extremes of wild hilarity
are found in life, and prizes

win no prizes." The smile was
put away. What have we done since then,
adult now and fleeced by circumstance,

by all that spiv morality, acquired
cheap? Our names are trenched and inked
in secret places. What we did

the cloakrooms brag of daily
to the changing boys. Each furtive
playground shed conceals a mis-

conception of the beauty that
we thought we'd ravish there. And then,
from dens of smoke and talk,

the teachers would emerge to say:
"You there. *Dilettante*. Doing everything
by starts and nothing long? *Who said that?*"

Our motto (did they too believe?)
was *rather of use than fame*, but in this
world that has no use for use

we learnt the fame of time,
"*Do not leave your seat*," they said.
Beyond the classroom window

the slow and sullen day
was building walls around our future.
"*Do not leave your seat.*"

We saw the future stumbling off
and watched it as a boy will watch a tramp
by the canal, then lob a stone.

Sit down! So you stayed seated.
Now and then would always be like this.
You held the stone. You learned.

Lübeck

The truth is, murmured Archimedes
I do not know what truth is.
How the wind howled that winter!
Rain scrubbed our tiles, scoured our
blank red faces. The truth is, as
we all know, that what we know
should not be confused with the truth,
perhaps . . .

    Archimedes shrugged. The
mediaeval gate had sunk between
two fingers of the glossy thorofare.
Christmas pinched each brick. The
water lay blackly in its own eyeball,
ruminant upon the cold. When I look
upon your naked body I am,

        Archimedes
glimpsed his sour reflection . . . *We*
are, he corrected, particles of the
same atom. The cars turn by all
night, through the rain. There is little
to choose between the cold of a winter
night and a cold heart. but we are
really,

    he coughed, it is my
conviction, he added, we are really,
as I am, tangled with you, et-
ernally warm on your breast, we are
really—and it is hard to say, no,
to put—*loving*. As I melted into the
grip of your legs and arms, the Baltic

flew frozen souls against me. Is
truth better than a compromise?

                        Yes,
said Archimedes, I think it is, no matter
that you do not know exactly in what
it consists. The cold might yet take you
over. Let us eat hot cabbage soup in
the unearthly light of fat women's
eyes, the fire and the clock will stroke
us. Let chimney-tops fall. I am
wrapped to a gradual understanding

                        of
what may be, your sweet skin. The
howl of motors on wet roads. The
distant and unmapped nightmare of
the heart's constraints put by. Your
breath, said Archimedes, is a sweet
summer night in my nostrils

                    though maybe
a storm in it somewhere, crashes
towards me like brutes through a wood.
I am, said Archimedes, aware of
these contradictions. Let the wind
flail out there, making such icy judgements.
I am, he added

        coming towards you.

Not a Description

It should always
be remembered
exactly, the fog
rising out of
warm fields

        and the peat-brown
        water.

    In the
    Fischerhütte
    I drank
    a *Pils*.

        Distances.
        A half-timbered church.
        The greenness of Lower Saxony.

At Cuxhaven
a green tug-
    boat,
a smell of oil,
    dead fish
        and sea.

        Out there
        is a greenness
        too.

Look!

The Portuguese navy
arrives for the *Kiel-
er Woche*, God
Bless them, all
suntanned
in the drizzle!

                       Down to Bremerhaven.

    Fidgets.
    Smell of the wind in
    long straight narrow lanes.
    Dykes and
        water   /   criss-cross
                      behind me
       deep in the heart of fields.

There is a loneliness.
If only I could get at it.
A true loneliness
            somewhere
around that corner.

Poplar trees. A rather
absurd girl playing
the flute to sheep.

                    You said
                    sound carries.

                    Horses galloping to Neuwerk,
                    across the mud.

> The flute
> and the fog.

What you will
never understand is how
the loneliness
tugs me away from you.

> *Bremer Kartoffelsuppe.*
> The coastline fell away to starboard.
> *Makrele Gebraten in Butter.*
> We set course for the Leeward Islands.

White smoke
drifting
mysteriously
into
trees.

The Secret

First I hid the village,
then I hid the sea.
Afterward, not telling,
there I put you and me.

Naked you lay there
between the dusty trees.
I swore the sky to silence
and crept between your knees.

There I locked the church,
the sanctimonious school,
falsified the map and re-
invented every rule.

Holding to each other,
clasped together there,
we lay in no man's land:
pink-tongued, bare-skinned,
                blonde-haired.

As waves came in and out,
the trees becalmed the sand.
The birds went round about
and atoms fizzed unplanned.

A struggle in the sky,
effortful, gave birth
again to what it was:
the fixed undoing earth.

So people found the place.
The guide book led them. "What
had we in mind?" they asked.
We stood and left the spot.

No matter how you fold
the score, the book, the map—
a riffling wind will blow
the pages gently back.

Song of the Grillbar Restaurant

Here is a song that I sang that was
sung in a place that was not song
which few are   and I kept an eye on myself
in the pink mirror
and the eye kept an eye on myself   and the coats

For here we had a glove with fingers
cruelly cut off   and here we had
pocketless coat, brimless hat, scarf with no throat
which I sang as follows
to be apart from you is death

I sang to this, the mantra of a folded mac,
O never do desert me, to the hooks
O see me through the worst, to walls of stale cream
I leave you now
and in the precious body of the cloakroom girl

I'll find a garmentless and maimed reprieve

Communications

Crimes of the pen and tongue
scatter their faults and flee
like evil children who see
no afterword, no wrong.

Lives out of language made—
accidents perhaps—
through flawed syntax
we enter chaos, much afraid.

But think of worlds of silence,
no struggle at the core,
beneath the tree of dumbness,
leafy shadows on the floor . . .

With no word for murder—
no name to call the act—
health is what we'd suffer,
the brutish force of fact.

Saying sickens saying
with its own disease—
the simple fact of being
wordier than need.

Poem

As the valley deepened, flowed to a curve,
and the river, pent, rose to a steep trill,
and the mountains before us hung in the sky,
and the road grew twisted and intractable,
a waterfall came tumbling from the blue rock
in a cool chute onto the road, and made
a small tributary we had to cross, stepping
over it, onwards going, and not looking back.

Later when the sun raided the afternoon,
we abandoned everything—hope, guilt, shame—
and the grass and earth tasted in our nostrils,
and a wild horse clouded where we lay.
He pawed at the rock, and his heavy dam
snuffled out of silence, eerily. Everything
waited as we plunged into an icy emptiness—
almost like water, curving out, a spout upon the air.

Who Invited Carstairs?

(1)

Carstairs arrived at the party
wearing his cape. Only his arm and leg

    protruded into the kitchen, where
    beer was being upended—
    people in oxygen masks
    going down into badinage.

  The chatter was stiff like a Christmas tree.
  Girls fell sideways onto sofas. Laughter. Heat.

I don't think I remember
Carstairs at all. Isn't he . . . ?

    The fact is, somebody was
    found slit open like a sack,
    presents for all the guests
    spilling out like blood.

  A gold cigarette lighter lit a gold-tipped
  cigarette and another lady exploded like a cork.

It was an awfully good
party. Carstairs must have

    slid through a hole in
    the planet or alternative
    out into some other dark
    where no one remembers him . . .

  I must remind you, sir, that anyone you kiss
  may be kept under surveillance for posterity.
  Who could have foreseen that? A razor-edged comb
  slicing open her head like an egg. People have been
  dying like photographs. All good clean healthy . . .

No such thing as fun
officer. Carstairs lies out
off the shore of Arcturus.
His taxi's waiting . . .

>Letters that may or may not come
>may not ever be sent. It's an illusion.
>Imagine Carstairs in a wide hat
>and artist's blue cravat. He painted on glass
>deferential portraits of the rich.
>Always about town. The wherewithal—
>the courage—to take the alleyways between
>gloomy women with sagging cigarettes,
>filthy bodices and pants. So tall, he . . .

Once in the country
I was reminded of Carstairs . . .

>He walked between the corn, always cheerful
>in long high boots. The party was really, you
>might say exceedingly . . . you only had to
>touch. Please touch. Going upstairs to
>
>>bedrooms I've not
>>visited yet, where
>>spectacles lie en-
>>twined. His spec-
>>tacles and hers upon
>>the bedside table,
>>they're not power-
>>ful enough to
>>even see the stars.

Carstairs never wore them. Eyes like a hawk.
Walked 20 miles a day. Wrote in the heat.
Had an encounter with Leibniz. Tripped

on a stump. Love's so completely far fetched . . .
Meanwhile someone was doing
a strip. Taking off everything:

>Only Carstairs' grub-like smile
>remained on the door. Somebody
>thought his replica of holy garments
>false to the latest event.

Brother who'd mounted his naked sister
in full view, we had been waiting for. No
conversation enacted any of our our cherished
realisms: they fell like ash behind the bookcase.

Become: We'd not yet become
the reproach we felt
Carstairs stood for. Of all
the people I talked to,
I don't think I knew who I was . . .

>One could have squeezed one's way
>along the mantlepiece, behind the clock.
>The records have it, the files, the whole
>registry dept. I am after all me. Is this clear?

And the corpse of the girl
who seemed to be just lying there,
nude, imperturbable, butchered,
as if she had just arrived . . . ?

(II)

Carstairs rarely spoke.
He sailed over the seas.
He sat in cafés.
He watched the clock.

He parted his trousers.
He ate no lunch.
His inscrutable stare.
He emptied the slops.
He swam in a river.
He painted the mayor.
He wrote no books.
He peered through a gap.
His unrequited love.

        Like swords the jealousies
        flickered and struck. Old
        hats and coats were discarded.
        The adage was mounted
        on carmined lips: this is
        our first generalisation:
        we have all been had.

Carstairs would never have participated
in such sensual foolishness. All de-
reliction of the spirit seemed to him
a dank twig. He was fired brick.
Red-skinned, athletic . . . degrees from Harvard, the
Sorbonne, the Whale, the Beetle, Avoirdupois.

    When shall we raise again
    the lips to the lips, clink heads?

  (III)

Carstairs is definitely laughing.
I've never seen the man. He
slipped correctly dressed
between the door jamb and
the door. His foot only
caught my eye.

When the party started to grow cool,
the lavatory flushed, the lonely tap . . .

Pausing on the stairs desperately one was
not distracted, not even entertained.

I've been trying to 0
visualise what it was.

I saw Carstairs' nose
in the waterjug,
aquiline, aristocratic,
ineffably present

(is there no remedy for what cannot
be diagnosed? He waved me goodbye . . .)

yet departing as though you or I
or the world itself would never
beheaded
come to this, though there are many who
speak after the act and smile
putting the executioner
at ease.

Carstairs has photographs
to prove he has snapped them at it.
At most of history
he stands behind his tripod,
measuring the light:
is that his flashbulb popping?

Carstairs has this to say:
"Move somewhat to the left . . ."

(Can you hear him? His voice
is faint as the wind. Brutal tones.
Harsh vowels. Bitter consonants.)

[52]

"Now stare alienated
off right centre, just
like that. There is no history
in this dead art. Personally
the most responsive subject is . . .
not nowadays to be obtained . . .

>(His fading laughter. A pair
>of trousers, checked, well-washed.)

"Dead or good, it's hardly
important. But dead at least
people will believe me. They've
nothing more to lose . . .
Why should I deceive you?
Death has just deceived itself."

>(Is that laughter . . . ?)

Long John Silver's Song

In my ivory sailor's heart,
wide fields of the sea unfold.
When the beat of the breakers starts,
the bell of my journey is tolled.

Girls, there were three
and the gluttonous mouth of the sea took them
and the starve-long acres of boredom
and time that was hung between sea and horizon.

In my ivory sailor's head
sea memories crash and spill.
The ivory, sea-interred dead
are barnacles on my will.

Girls, there were three
and their skeletons dance in a shanty of loss
to the wind's bright tune, on a tress of hair,
and a diamond glitters in each dead eye.

In my ivory sailor's soul
the shape of a thunderstorm grows.
An augury rides on its roll:
the crowblack sail a gypsy knows.

Girls there were three
and I stole what I stole from each one
and the surf ghosts over the sand
and whispers a kiss and is gone.

In my ivory sailor's heart
wide fields of the sea unfold.
When the beat of the breakers starts,
the bell of my journey is tolled.

A Moment of Truth in *Le Bar Du Château*

Canals ruminate on spoiled air,
gluttonous and placid. I love
ships, dung and water—credulous
emotions sparking on rubbish.

The trees are mute, the blowsy
water glooms. Along the path: *Le Bar
du Château* and a slattern griping
from the doorway into deadening afternoon.

"*Bonjour!*" "*Bonjour!*" Thank God it's empty.
Tables and pinball and the barman, his
grotesquely fleshy arms upon the counter,
anchoring the Sunday paper with tattoos.

Headlines: *J'adore Jésus Christ!
La Sainte Vierge est ma Copine!* In turbid
eyes his soul skulks like a pike, toils
to raise salvation in a glass of *Meuse*.

The paint drips. Plastic table cloths
urge retreat. The slut enfeebles me;
I'm devoured with belief, necessity of dirt,
the callous come-on, the easy-perfumed breath.

Rain rots through leafless branches.
Sucking air, the ruined water swells
to marvellous dimensions, pouring through
the hull, clutching the keel, gulping

through the portholes: all is distended
in this vile bladder. I am in love
helplessly. Chairs, tables, beer glasses,
I kiss you all, as tears stain my cheeks.

To the God of Creative Writing

Dear   friendly
smiling   brass   god

I think you
know what is good

You look to me
like a god who has read

a lot of books
from where you lean against the wall

Is it my fancy
that with each book you read

your smile grows broader?
I'm pleased you travel with me

in my luggage
packed   unpacked

on a shelf   on the table
You came with me from Africa

I don't think Europe
surprised you

I owe you
thanks for reminding me

of what it is
I'm trying to do

and occasionally
when I hit my dynamite keys too hard

and you fall over
with a thunk

it reminds me
that creation, like love-making

sometimes ends up
in funny positions

Money

You lisna me.
A poet gotta have lotsa money.
Lotsa lotsa money. Fancy cars. Beautiful
                     and O so expensive ladies.
In fact, the works.
Why only then
Will he be able to write down
The little thoughts, the wee tiny invisible O
                           so unimportant thoughts
That for all their infinitesimal nature
Are really H U G E !

yes.

And if a poet, to show off, wanna buya monkey,
                     he should
Be ablea buya monkey, no problem,
                         cash down.
So long-tailed swinging monkey
Leap from anglepoise lamp to self-built
                        structural furniture
Tipping Pisas of poetry into the trash.
Gibber gibber, little monkey hands
Mocking intelligent big scribblers,
O the priceless and purchasable irony of it!

And wella monkey costa lotta money.
Needa expensive house to put a monkey in!
Just walk right out and buya house
Half-sunken by the sea with
                           aquamarine living room,
Big shark watching you eat breakfast
And bills coming in like the tide,
While poet get out Super V-8 air-conditioned white-wall

                          laureate-lined hi-fi motor car
And go to absolutely no work you
                          betcha,
Leaving monkey
To show funny rosy bottom to the shark
Ha!

A poet oughta get lotsa money
                    for each poem.
Like, I mean, lotsa money, you would be
                              surprised,
So he can financy flimflam and buya cheetah
Make re-make of *The Iliad* in Blindoralpoetryscope
And having put film in can
Poet go home with cheetah and two equally fast-moving pets,
Sit in Japanese garden with picture-window'd pleasure-drome
Sipping white syrup and cane rum
Glancing through the eyepiece of his ten million
                         magnification telescope
At the edges of the known universe
While his pets strip to their appendix scars
And play brutalising scenes on the tender swing
And the ex-chef of the President of the French Republic
Make *Baked Beans á la Piscine Municipale* on toast
And over each other's bloombright bodies a lot of
                    extras are smearing tomato sauce
While the cheetah is eating the Japanese petunias.
Our poet, however, has
Altogether gone
Upstairs to a plain simple room
Writing: *Dear Mum, Since I wrote to you last week I've been thinking*
         about what you said about what Dad said and it has distracted me
         so much my astronomy has suff . . .

Well, I mean, with poets pulling down
                        a monthly income like that
All the stockbrokers would be living on
                        cheap red wine
And cycling to Wall Street for the love of the Bourse
And their girl-friends, removing perfumed knickers,
                        would say:
I admire I really admire a man
                who is prepared to give up so much
To get that portfolio which out-performs the rest
I mean, who just loves the abstract mathematics of it—
I mean it makes you realise, these poets,
                with their fancy houses
                        in Palo Tenor Saxophono,
All that piling up words just for the sake of it,
Scrambling over each other to get
                        le mot juste
Well, it makes you realise, as I
                        suddenly do
(Hurriedly replacing knickers)
That I could give up a man who has given up so much
(Hurriedly replacing bra)
Go out and look for someone who has
                        so much to give up for
I mean a poet! A real poet!
Not a self-denying worm like you!
(Slam!)
But the poets, alas, and quite frankly
Are living examples of the truth of that old adage
Never Chase Bees in the Nude
For there is a pale brown-haired beauty
In love with truth, freedom, Spanish guitar, white walls, imagination
The right to be oneself unless

Of course, it is to be *The Other Marilyn Dobbs*,
In love with poverty, high seriousness, the right to privacy
And prayer with a whiff of marijuana smoke that calms the air,
And she is quietly-read and well-spoken and not at all
                            hung up about being a priestess of sex,
And she comes to you fascinated by cheetahs and monkeys
                                      and expensive stuff
And offers you her knickers with the charitable smile of a saint
And you say: "Listen, babe,
I know it's not my beautiful body and my incredible wealth
You're after,
It's my mind, the inner me. So scram."
And she goes sadly, truly attracted by your body and your money.
And you sit at the mirror
And put out your tongue at the troll who is watching you
And let your little thoughts, those
                         tiny, exquisite pearls beyond price
Trit trot across the rackety bridge of your mind.
Such a cunning face. Such a clever troll. It
Brooks no excuses, devours them one by one.
IDIOT!   *FOOL!*   *YOU WILL GET WARTS!*

Time and Western Man

Rubbish in the alley
Rubbish in the heart
Is this the human opera?
Better make a start . . .

Lie upon the sofa
Stare into a void
Girls are always talking
Boys are soon annoyed

That was the misfortune
You mistook the queue
Stood in line for ages
Ended up with you

I was here before you
You were here before
They were here before us
Before is still the law

Nick, the king of daydreams
Nell, the queen of need
Tell you that they love you
Love's a funny creed

Experience the present
Just like yesterday
Tomorrow is tomorrow
This must be today

Rip the date off quickly
Use your naked wit
Seize the moment slowly
Make the best of it

The Dwarf

I live at the top of a deserted tower.
I'd hoped to see the sea, but there's a hill in the way.
When I leave, you'll regret it.

I'm cutting a chicken's throat. A seven-
year-old girl is watching me anxiously. She's
next, if I don't decide to be nice.

I like to plunge my arm up to the elbow
into the bowels of a horse. In my red cap you'd
take me for a professor of scatology.

I don't like this situation much. I'd like
to work for a friendly farmer and be his black dog.
Something is tearing in my gut.

I'm harmless. Really I am. Couldn't you
hear me last night? I killed a child and a cat in my dream.
I wept so much I am blind today.

There are three hundred and twenty seven
steps in this tower. I'm going downstairs with the key.
My hair is agitated, as if by wind.

A slit in a doorway admits no-one, nor allows
departure. I know that my presence likewise embarrassed you.
I am trotting, hunched, over the hill and away.

Farewell!
You'll be sorry!

The Dentist

Mouths. Open mouths.
I'd like
to padlock them.
I keep seeing
souls
lodged there:
tattered, untended,
not properly
treated.

Once a soul flew
right out and
into me. Under
my white coat
two souls fought it out,
then merged into
radiant pabulum. I
can see an inch wider
on both sides.

Sometimes I find them
on the surgery floor,
trampled and thin—
like communion wafers.
I use them to mark
the pages
of my pharmacopoeia.

Other souls
hang shyly back,
skulk in the pharynx.
With my stalk-mirror
I read them:
*"We have no fear

*but this body
is craven. It is
mud here. All mud,
terrible, dark poll-
uting mud."*

I busy myself with teeth—
little white simulacrums
of the soul. I drill,
puff air, inject my wads
of dental cement,
prepare another set
to masticate the world.
and all the while
the souls pop up and down
like numerals
in the window
of a cash register:
    "Who are you?"
    "Can you help us?"
    "We are lost?"
    "Is this
    the way out?"

It's a terrible life
being a dentist.

My Friend Moultby

I went down the street to see Moultby,
Moultby was lying on his back, in the air.
His attic let in no light. I said:
"Moultby, you are levitating."
He said:

> "You are a disgusting poet.
> I'm trying to outfloat Freud
> and Marx and the rest of that gang.
> We must all stop being such
> animals. We should all try to be nice
> to each other, like flowers."

I rolled a cigarette and smoked it.
Moultby went very slowly up
and down by a sheer effort of will.
I said: "Moultby, you'll tire yourself."
He said:

> "What are friends for
> if not to watch other friends
> tire themselves? I'm trying
> to revoke society from
> the bottom upwards. Let
> us use constructivism and hope!"

I thought for a while of
the swine who sell stale tobacco.
Nothing's for much in this world.
I said: "Moultby your attic's a microcosm!"
He said:

> "You're just a fool. No
> effort in you. I'm all
> effort. We shall only
> save ourselves by floating,
> not by your absurdities
> in verse, improbable rhymestering!"

Such an effort of con-
demnation Moultby made of
poetry he forgot to levitate.
Came down with a crash.
Said:
> "Frankly I think I've broken
> My back. Anything you can do? I wish
> the ceiling was more interesting.
> Why don't you help me up?"

Lament for the Subotica-Palić Tramway

Let's have a lament for things past.
It's easy to do and it costs nothing:
Let's get down to how things
      really ought to be.

On a Sunday afternoon the trams used to run
Out along the edge of the maize-fields
With windows open, so that the dark men in
      white shirts
And the softly-interior-smiling women with
      high-buttoned necks
Could feel the breeze, the aromatic air, as
      it soothed their sweat.
And the tram used to roll along its weedy track
At ten miles an hour; the chocolate-brown tram
That came to a halt every two hundred yards
And sat in the patient silence of emptiness
While others climbed aboard. How different this was
From the modern horror, the ghastly contemporary
      totalitarian ear-drum pounder,
The never-silent always-polluting high-tyred
              motor-bus!

When the tram stopped, everything stopped.
And then you would hear the clunky sound of the bell,
Halfway between a ding and a thud,
And the tram would slip backwards a little,
      preparing itself,
And then clout you in the back with enormous
      electric acceleration
Till it reached a speed somewhat above walking pace!
The people loved it, for it always stopped for them.
It carried fat ladies ten feet and then placed

      them down on the earth again
With their bags and double-chins and the worries
      that fat ladies have.
And the conductor would sometimes let it go on
      to the next stop
While he finished a conversation with a friend
      encountered in the street.
Then, with a jolting run, his dull-colour'd
      mechanical clipper
Knocking his breast-bone, he would rejoin
      the ship!
And the tram would go through the town in its
      special sanctuary of track,
Along an aisle that had been laid down for it,
Rather as a file of monks, in a religious age,
Might pass with regularity, quite unobserved,
      through a busy populace.
And the people in the street could hear its
      vibrato-less bell
As it went by, a reminder of gentle motion, of
      the agreeable flux of affairs,
Without turmoil or passion or agitation.

After the tram ran the school-children, or hung
      off the back step,
Or clustered in the standing place round the doors,
Never deigning to occupy the narrow and immensely
      polished wooden seats,
But rolling with the warps in the track, feeling
      the sensation of something precarious but solid.
And it was a single-track line, that tramway,
With passing places, at every third stop.
You waited while the contrary tram came

        slowly up the line to meet you,
Its big beetle front swaying and glittering,
Taking, O an appreciable swathe of time from
        the fortunate afternoon,
Until it swung alongside and you gazed at the
        contrary people, sitting in silence,
Smiling, perhaps, at their own absurd contrariety,
        until
With a bound you were off again
        down that track.

And leaving the town in the summer, the air was
        heavy with the dust of crops.
People with huge water melons sat, leaning forward,
        gazing across the flatland.
And sometimes, I've been told, the chocolate tram would derail,
        at its usual unspectacular pace,
And plough gently into the maize, nesting its large
        iron buffers
In the stiff green-shirted plants, with their pale
        yellow cobs.
And the whole tramway of the town would come to a
        stop,
While an extraordinary breakdown wagon, of cables and
        winches, and a small crane,
Would come out of the house where all the trams
        spent the night
And wallow towards the crisis point, with officials in
        uniform
Standing on either side. Meanwhile the rest of the trams
        did not move.
They could not advance or retreat, and so people
        would say:

"The tramway's broken down!"
And the occupants of each tram would step out
        and conversation would flower under the plane-trees
In the centre of the town. And some would decide to walk,
But others would not be so pressed.
And even in the case of a winter's day
People would warm themselves with talk,
        remaining inside,
And feel themselves pleasantly marooned.

Of course the old tramway grew old.
New buses came from Sweden and gave the streets
        a new look.
But it was not long before they began to look
        dusty and grubby and somehow chewed-up.
And it seemed that they were always late, or you had just
        missed one,
Or they were impossibly crowded. And between each
        stop
Was a huge distance,
So that the fat ladies were carried almost as far
        on the wrong side
As they got on the right side.
And finally they closed the tramway altogether
Which, I believe, was the cause even for tears
        among some folk,
To see those old chocolate beetles stacked like so
        many boxes
In the single-roomed mansion from which they had once
        so proudly lumbered forth
To serve the people. And nobody really knew what
        to do with them,
So they are still there to this day, rusting and rotting,

With the wood ripped away and the windows shattered,
All their once priceless character now derided,
And even the landmarks of their route
Are torn up, except
For a few strands of track, embedded here and there
        in the cobbles.

It was a woeful day
When they closed the tramway, and I wish to sing
Of my deep surprise and astonishment,
(And of my deeper knowledge that this
        is always so,
But nevertheless to sing)
Of my profound sadness, my uneasiness of mind,
That we should leave fat ladies standing at the tram-stop
        gazing sadly into distant rain.

And I will sing ...

Ten Poems for Treasure

MEETING

From different ends of the city prosodic squalls of wind and evening light tap like knuckles at the window of the heart. A *rendezvous* is a pitiless thing.

Shadows from dark corners. An old man is a moonless hesitation. His age is weary as a finger. Concentrating on the great muscle of his heart, he feels the god within him, dark as his own blood. In ritual chairs, seated, he throws off Latin phrases, sardonic gloves. No one could forgive him. His corrupt tactics blend cardinally with the purple and crimson.

I see myself poised between lovers. Through rained-on gleams of pavement, through gutterpools and peelings, he slips between the withheld favours of the night. She crosses a soaked garden, the boughs brush her forehead, her coat open, her bag undone. The gate opens and a cello, *arco*, plays three notes.

In a dead window, a candle flickers. Soul-burglars, robbing the moon-grey clouds of silver, they are warding off time beneath a tattered sky. I am almost inclined to believe in them. I hear their storms of words. I hear the thrashing of wind-ruffled shrubs in the ghostly park.

To take precise bearings is hardest of all. To see there is no course, yet take one. To hold the rudder fast where maps dissolve on shores of rumour. To watch the darkness suddenly reveal an opening and ask yourself—is this the threshold?

What lies beyond?

Before the stagnant reaches of a settled lake, the lovers stand and watch as age breaks upward through the surface, his ghastly face aglow with tears and regrets, the water cascading round him.

I see my brothers and my sisters, all contained within their own anxieties, unreachable beyond the love that milks my throat. I see the opacity of cubes and squares. They have dimension and space and volume enough to crowd me, pleading, against the few words of light that come tenderly down.

She is absolute and daring, a falling shiver of brilliance in a vesper sky. You would think they would reach forever towards each other across those unbridgeable rivers of trash and filth, those moody and turbulent currents, the decomposing fragments of the world. But no. They are walking away bodily into distinct and separable darkness, heading inexorably back towards the garish and multitudinous and anxious cosmos.

Like A Game of Draughts

Now she is smoking. Blue exhalations. They mount steeply the sides of a porcelain bowl, caress the rim and pour thickly inside to stir the dried flowers she has placed there.

From her half-raised casement, a London square is seen to be occupied, a stride of refusal. Sunlight jumps and takes it. When she closes her eyes the buildings are removed.

Observe how her strong profile is queened, white and black in her motion, her tender pain. I feel the resilience of despair, in her, in me, endlessly extensible, taut. We must advance into the springy area of combat or in the passive domains of self-protection we shall be picked off, one by one.

Children imitate life at hopscotch. Within this sober room, their voices grow rowdy and cruel at her shoulder.

She thinks of the recommencement of the game. Pacing the spectators, the crises, the silken foulards, the attentive and O so lonely players, she thinks of the dreams that make the children run and laugh.

She is as unsure of herself as I am, yet her ruthlessness mocks from a mirror.

Is it in her egotism that the strong hard shapes of want move alternately like draughtsmen?

There is only the certainty that life must contain her—*bellicose princess* or *queen of contemptible rhapsody.*

She snarls and rears her naked form; shadows of foliage play across her breasts and stomach. She whimpers and the dark crevice of her sex fills with illusions and dreams.

Huffed.

Fall

The fragments of autumn lean like trees into the shuddering, lilac, rainy morning.

Beds are turned back, their sheets have lost us; their pillows bear no imprint or remembrance. The sad dust of summer trickles along gutters.

Veils descend, of rain, of melancholy afternoons, of old and holy light. Walking beneath umbrellas, those who come face to face with love and cannot breathe turn ineffectually into shop doorways.

Tube-trains gasp open and shut, exuding the freshly damp odour of clothes. The trains jerk into motion and the brows of the people cross with their hesitant tragedies.

Over the rooftops the airplanes whine. Lamp-posts turn greener, sprucer. In the fallow coral-brown tennis courts, lagoons of water collect and lie at random. Feel how the ghost of traffic lurks in the warm, wet emptiness of roadways, how the houses savour their memorabilia, conferring their silence and uniquely similar remarkableness on pots, tiles, windows, doors.

Notice the suspicion with which our future regards us, crossing the park.

Quarrels of the year succour our mythic reflections.

We are in a great bowl, highly polished, skateboarding against the sides. We gather speed to run up, climb, and at the apogee of our momentum turn, pause, and come spinning down.

Leaves chatter and slip from their stems.

We are in a great bowl, lilac and rainy.

Churchbird

In the deception of philosophy a caged owl waits.

In the ruins of reason creep the mice.

With all your imperatives you can still do nothing. Taking the uneasy bird upon your finger you find yourself within the precincts of a speechless house. What more is possible? Tears cannot ail you or cure you. Before the bewildering mystery you are merely a droplet of wax, moving in slow descension along the slender, white-gold column of the offertory candle.

There are shapes and voices in the distance that you can see and hear but not make out, for the infinitely tall window lets in pictures only, crimson, blue and green, colouring the dullness where saints crowd to the rail. You can hear their childish *oohs* and *aahs*. Steadily you look upon the gas of the soul, burning in its brass cup.

The bird blinks. A lion nuzzles your empty palm.

It is too faraway. What is felt and seen and lovingly required occurs as if, somewhere at the back, somewhere in the claustral box of your confession, somewhere in a book or in the drapes of long-unmoved belief, a voice made you look up.

The vaulted roof. A whirling.

You flinch away from coruscating wings. The bird ascends.

Ascends.

BAWDIFUL

Running a brothel I see myself doing something useful.

In my high-ceilinged hallway, clients will pause embarrassed before the tangible resurrection of their fantasy. A multiplicity of doors. My attentiveness.

Behind each door is Susy. All the lethargies of the flesh.

To sadness, and to the discharge of ungrandiose passions, to the inexorable consummations of helpless and painful desires—I am like a fly, living from the offal of the heart.

To the gentle inadequacies of a dream finally exposed, to the lifting of soiled garments, to the hurtless instruments of love shown to be as they really are, to the blue eyes that have looked so long, and without longing, into the hapless features of lust—to all these I am thoughtful probity and understanding.

When the vile uniforms of the upright come by for a free copulation and a reading of the regulations, Susy will stand beside me, her bought soul glowingly naked. They will muddle, in panic, their fatuous rubric of justice and morality.

Susy will smile. The smile of prostitution is the eagle of the abyss.

I will build my brothels in the ashes of family. I will eat my meals backwards and grapple with the monstrosities of the people. Everyone will be welcome: lizards, dwarves, mendicants. I will scale the walls of their fatalistic castles, admit myself through incredibly narrow apertures to the turret chamber where their demon is imprisoned. Not with a sword, but with a dream, I will lead them to momentary rest.

See where my buildings stand.

They are dull brick structures. They have many windows and many doors. They roll away into the distance and over the curve of the horizon.

Nothing else resembles them. They are what they are.

BARBARIAN

O Dr Prinz, why did you try to kill music for me?

You are dead now. I passed your house. I stood before its brutal cadaver—virulent Jewish-German barrack of your tortoise soul—and my senses were exiled.

In Celtic rows we tortured lives of great composers into copperplate. Between the lines of the stave we looped and whorled our alphabets, and our resentment made us deafer than Beethoven.

With my dumb, plug-ugly hatred I became a Philistine. Walking bloody and embattled fields I slew the faint and beautiful prayers of the dying. A cold melody became an insult to my warmer self. In its fading intricacy all language seemed to me nothing but a scurrilous drone for mercy. Through the morgue of words, I lumbered with bound feet, with over-languid breath.

The whole world supported me. We found sticks and truncheons. We gathered at the mansion gates. Through the rusty ironwork we jeered and yelled. Was it, could it have been, the house of relapsed time? Our faces were ablaze as we awaited movement that would gratify our vain malignity.

Look and measure the crudeness of this body! Observe this barbaric cavorting! These leaps! These stamps! These shakes!

There is no fairness or beauty in what pomposity, arrogance, puerile conviction, undoubtingness, may make of a child. To become hot, intractable and foolish is the mark of indelible resultingness.

Your calculated joviality, Dr Prinz, was a knife at the throat of my horn.

Breakdown

Now there are the disturbances of form, the seismic undergoings which alter the ordinary stable shapeliness of things. In motion the senses are put to doubt and the heart is swimless.

At a breakdown she turned blue and her tongue lodged in her heart and stopped it. I loved her eyes. Childish and shattered by the enormous pressure of vital urges, she flew off into fragments. The windows, doors, vases, needed their faces slapped.

What could you do against it? Sensationally extended sobs forced their way to the top. Brutalised against the washbowl, mercy spits out broken teeth—the water flows. So? Love is misplaced. The sea's ferocious weight will bend the spirit. *O sea of love!* The planet's own unease is in the very nerves of you!

Elemental messages. A billion tons of water rear up and crack against another equal weighted wave. That whole tympanic motion stuns to a colossal standstill—paralysed. A massiveness of depthless surging, calamitously met!

When everything is gone, the stars and the birds will fly upwards, away from the peaks of the earth. They will fly in a long coo of resentment to places where no great travail may bite them. They will hop and jostle in dowries of light and harmony while, far off, growling unutterably, the sea will pace the shore and the earth's drum, in the background, will roll.

Starcrux

The stars rail at decency. Their cosmic messages flow into the sense of the world; my motion transfuses with silver heat. Leaning towards my own reflection, dark, four-pointed, featureless, I watch it rise from unequalled water.

Ghost of identity, you are more real to me than my self. You have conquered emotion. No longer will you strut in the mire of your disequilibrium, or topple, ungravitied, towards the centre of a woman. Starlight glitters in you, acclaims you, as your shadow—astrally empierced—falls to meet the black surface of the pool.

What insults, what rejections this cheap suitcase full of blood and mad memories and useless muscle had to endure in earth-like silence! Women and men who lied to each other in the failed spirit of an atheist's deathbed prayer! Love that came cautiously out of a tight fist! Words meant to please, carrying the ribbon of death with them! Contemptible, sycophantic, toadying pettinesses! Urgent authority, alarumed with its megalomania! Love that went whimpering back into a hole!

Only a scavenger of stars could perceive what the sky might brood in the long marvel of stormlight. Chinking money for beer in his hand, he walks through spectral boulevards with dung on his jacket, straw in his eyes. Abused, forced to the naked and damnable stallionry of cobbled yards, clutching the appeased words of the savagely satisfied, his arrogant abasement masters the hopeless. Ragged, bleeding with radiance, he steps with contempt over the bread-warm bodies of the comfortable. He will pause only at the edge of this regarding world.

Rain in his shoe! The earth accosts him! Spits on him!

He is like the still, silent walk of the moon's shadow, passing from midnight.

We are into the eclipse, into the deluge, the murmured come of the fall.

Now the stars, by one, by two, emerge to gradual and smiling celebration.

Treasurepoem

Long John Silver, Bluebeard, Captains Bligh, Blackjack and me are all assembling in one mutinous concentration of fever upon a parrot-torn beach. The surf reveres us like a blind beggar feeling a naked prostitute. Abscessed tree-logs, eaten-out corpses of vast fish, murderous tendrils, all grope and thresh in a flotsam of agony on the miraculous sand. The vegetation, the tracks and rivers, the volcanoes and clouds beyond, all emit in chorus their high-pitched signal of unease. Reel and die, island. Reel and die.

We are as filthy as our hot dreams. We have sailed a million years through story-books, fornicating out of sight, behind the print. When no children were looking we slit the gullets of merchants to procure their secret maps. Profound is our revolution. We have overthrown the state of the heart.

Progress was treachery. To devour our ends we lied ourselves straight with dissembling. We shocked God with semi-literate barings of monstrous breasts, with phenomenally dishonest professions of love and courage.

Taking our hooked knives we cut the sanity of the island to pieces, ripping the foliage of slumbering philosophy, executing dogs, assassinating monkeys. The warm brown streams of thought are turned to flailing hysteria. We ford the rivers with make-shift barges hacked from idealistic trees. From our fervour, the moral fish perish. We piss, howling at each other, into Paradise.

There are to be rocks and stony uplands. The map shows that in the heart, the most dangerous place of all, the fire-soul of the island, treasure that no man saw or believed is waiting to be taken.

Now we have still murdered each other, believing each of us is nearer to the guilty fire.

I am climbing down into the volcano, my teeth sharpened on human flesh, my rapacity barbed in every point, my eyes sharp from the whetstone of struggle, my body cracking its tight skin, my blackguard hands like pikes.

Well, and what did you find there?

If there is to be an end to this story it is nothing, for no story ends.

If solutions are what you look for, pull your pillow over your head and suffocate. This is no time to bother someone like me.

If it is the inexorable question-mark you seek, the ineffable *what*, no report can possibly be audible within the roaring, belching fountain of the inmost fire. Flames. O yes, naturally there are flames, and a terrible updraught of unrelenting and revengeful force. The centre has been set entirely alight. Watch, now, the hideous bonfire, famished for miracles, famished for hope.

These are my ashes of strength.

Read in my eyes and requite.

Love is the only princess who makes plots. She is the wheel of the story; she unfolds from the kernel of all fire and her hair kisses her cold flesh, and the forms of her body, kissed with flame, are numerous as death.

She is like you but she has no answer.

She is the end of the dotted line, the X, the only violator.

She is the *nihilo*, the O, the zero, the absolute.

She is what every island protects, what we have rampaged across, what no feet upon the sand have ever touched or reached.

In the silence and mystery of all-deafening conflagration.

Better no end than no end.

The Bird

Across a once-unfortunate web of streets memory strode out with a hunting-bird on each taloned fist.

Knowledge of love's absence is the gentle but unsuitable prompter of disquiet.

During that progress there were carnal rumours flying from door to door, so that the young men met you with smiles on their forgiving faces.

Suffering is here distilled in the broad curve of a green avenue. An intersection is like a migraine. The face of the underground station is like someone you know.

When the rain and the clouds gather at a crossroads I see you walking towards me out of time. People nod to us and greet us, though they could not have seen us before. People seen only in dreams look familiar.

The whole city is like a headscarf you wear round your throat.

I think our feet upon the pavements must be heard in the silent second-storey rooms that look down upon us. I seem, not entirely, though I also seem to be trying, not entirely to grasp your hand or your intention.

The bird flew off.

See where it is still aloft. Over the precincts of the town.

When the quarry is finally located, it will sink down with burning speed into the intolerable city.

And it will call out.

Call out.

The Ship

The light weakens toward death.
Changes are bred in time.
Out of the chalice, the silver bud,
the frame of energy holds the line.

Mazes. Stars. A clean abstraction
lights the world with gleaming rivers.
Forests, mountains vanish out of sight.
Emptiness the dream delivers.

Change from absence lets
the heart know truth it can't admit.
The next requirement is: look.
The dark is close to where you sit.

Here in time the form of it:
a chair, perhaps, a mask, a loom?
A woman combing pale hair?
The devastation of a room?

Where you touch or lean, the light
is faltering. Vibrations mount
within the vacancy. Brilliant structures
shatter beyond count.

Will repetition free or kill?
The world's a symbol, always loss.
Its lines and holy congruences
fall beneath the hush of frost.

Too late there will be penances.
The cries and damages will warn.
Too late. And then the birds will move
away across the sky to dawn.

And this exemplary, unbeaten ache,
this yearning outward like a ship
will curve in white trajectory to stars
that hold it silvered in their grip.

Flea Market

I'd like to think that lovers walk
on water. Or think deep thoughts.
But this is no place for a liar.
We are the poor, Paddy and I;

let me wear this disguise.
The wind shunts cloud from hope to hope.
A breezy day, and if I could be wise
I'd be careful, I'd be clever—

but here we are standing by our stumps of stones,
twenty-three pairs, some odd,
of shoes, and a picture of God—
his God, not mine, and Paddy's bones

which we're endeavouring to sell:
Paddy take your skin off.

Four Seasons

(ACT ONE)

. . . urial?

Under shabby planes
                a driveway
winds
     through drifting foliage
of the estate

Days
   bear
misty
   edges of the year

Footsteps cross the gravel
sunshades have been taken in

Plates no longer clatter in the kitchen
children have run off into the trees

Two sit there
drinking wine without speaking
not touching

She doesn't smile

Her blouse unbuttoned to the waist
she slides a jewelled wrist inside
strokes herself for him, watching
holds his regard, gently

Leaves flirt with the wind . . .
a breeze, maybe, the scion
of the falling year appoints
yet he appoints no followers

Fire eats the straw
air feeds on smoke

From lengths of meadow and ditch
the self-confessing gust
darts this way and that against the grass . . .

She peels the shirt back
draws her shoulders up, offers him
encupped within the blades of slender fingers / what
stirs him, dirt beneath her nails
stirs him more than the frail swing
of her breasts

Red peppers hang on the outhouse wall
red peppers tile the roof,
red peppers droop over gutters
a mass of ochre, a harvest of flame

> *I have no further use for my self*   (she says)
> *what you ruled was myself*
> *what you do not rule, therefore*
> *attends my dissolution*

(ACT TWO)

Those who come with a petition through the storm
arrive late, at dusk
having ridden two miles down the frozen lake
(where skaters bow the ice like sheets of steel)
kick their boots against the wall
regretting their journey
turn heads to listen

To a cry that falls
from a high window

In a room beneath the eaves
he explores the pearl of her body
with tongue and sense

From the rounded strength of her upper legs
to where the skin trembles and opens

She jerks
and noiseless planks detach and topple from a parapet
she eases
and the plunge scatters powder everywhere
she shudders
and he males to her body as a tree to foggy light

The autos are at standstill on the wrecked highway
Priapus the God, muscle on muscle

Lights in the far city, blinking at nothing
lights in the far city, making no sense

A frost wind, tumbled and mixed with darkness
sweeps over maize-fields

> *Under the snow, Daddy*
> *things aren't cold, are they?*

> *No, child*

> *Daddy,*
> *why is it so silent?*

> *The element of snow, child*
> *is silence*

Stripped of sleep's
pleasurable fleece
her long hair
is dragged over pillows

A clock of whiteness
spinning through the night
drives time before it

> *Daddy! Daddy!*
> *everything looks different now*
> *will it still be the same*
> *underneath?*

> *I don't know, child*
> *I don't know*

(ACT THREE)

Plumped bolsters hang like sick tongues
from every window to air
and it is not possible to determine if
on tour of inspection / of state
or, say, released from the dead circuitry
he is not
       sitting on the kerb
his feet in the road
              by some
observed to have vaulted
a fallen tree in the park

There are people who are delighted
                        with his incalculability

    New sunlight prowls
    the green yard of the estate

    The long alley of trees
    suddenly fills with horses, riders

The puzzle jumps to life
while the old arrangement is still known
in the composition of its breaking-up

    They canter through leaves
    whipped by a squall of rain

    The alley empties
    pools shiver with reflected movement

He is everywhere
glittering and hurried in contempt and gesture
proud   negative   flying   light   brimming

She rides with him
he wants her dishevelled, she keeps herself that way

His sarcasm knows impossible variations
he wants her, he does not want her

But in private he comes to her, trembling. He
spreads disturbance within his web

It is the prerogative he claims:
to obey his own not carefully understood whim

(ACT FOUR)

Merlin remarks :

This is a gas-balloon
within a larger gas-balloon
    and so on
all rising, all moving
upwards and yet
    absolutely stationary

The king
is playing jacks
inattentive to his lesson
a bright   colloquial   sort of game

In the frame
of library windows
a flock of geese
wobbles past

Who could bear it?
the thrall of passion?

Under the roof of the granary
he had seen her big nude toes
which gripped the wagon-ruts
had taken those dirty feet into
his hot mouth

A failure of attention
and all his craving

The old counsellor and magician
is becoming frustrated :

Let us suppose
    the universe a gas-balloon
might that not too
    contain itself
within
    a gas-balloon . . . ?

Royalty's face wears
a deep flush of impatience :

Quiet Merlin!

If he had bitten them off

unable to run
she would have put down roots
deep into the soil

She would have possessed him
through his own eagerness

*Much better
to take a philosophical view*
                    says Merlin gently

You should bury me the king says

No, no
        says Merlin
a gas-balloon . . .
        and stops to stare

Those eyes, that mouth
so weak under strong light
were they not already
beginning to fade?

Had the king not ordered
his own b . . . ?

My Father was an Interventionist

One day on our grim walk to school—he to his, I to mine—
I saw a woman in a dressing gown, half-hanging from a window.
She was screaming, I assumed, because she was about to be murdered
and sure enough a dim figure behind pulled her back from the window
and gave her such a smack across the chops, she folded like an ironing board.
My father thrust his briefcase into my hand—"*Here, hold this,*" he said—
and dashed into the house, the front door of which, I remember,
stood interestingly ajar. A milk float stopped nearby
and the milkman eyed me—9 years old—and my too-manly briefcase
and made a cockney joke as he wandered past with his little hand-crate
    of pints,
while I stood in the treeless avenue listening for the sound of shots,
for the stentorian "*Take that!*" of my father,
or possibly a slow cortège of black Ford Pilot V8 automobiles
to slide up the street, and a sepulchral type in a top hat to step out of the
    first,
bow to me, and file with his dandruff-flecked assistants into the house,
or, better still, a squad of police to arrive in their jingling Wolseleys,
or a kind and significantly unmotherly lady to come down the drive,
draw me by the hand into the dark house and explain with gesture and
    illustration
what it was men and women did to each other alone in big houses
on broad streets like Mapesbury Road, with its gas lamps
and bunkers containing sand (for whatever purpose),
along which I walked, not holding my father's hand, every morning to
    school,
bored and frightened by the day's shadowy length in front of me,
doing that unformulated worrying a child does and asking myself why
when suddenly a drama took the stage, it should be so spectacular,
problematical even, and why it should involve my father
who was not even heroic to me? At any rate, I have to report
that after a while he returned silently,

took his briefcase, and we walked on wordlessly, faster than before,
his face rather pale, his suit unruffled, and me all of a question mark
to which, of course,—that was his style—he was not going to respond,
and only years later, it must have been years later,
it was several weeks, or millennia anyway,
he told me it was not advisable to intervene in a quarrel
between a man and a woman, because they both
turn on you with the conjoined fury they have previously
and singly reserved for one another. And this is not good.

On First Looking into Gittings' 'Keats'

Disturbing to find, as I reach a distant page,
my father's notes on odd-sized scraps of paper.
I squint, deciphering his fine-gauge
scrawl, my father's ever-parsimonious, tapered,
margin-crawling stabs at what he meant.
But truthful and exact. I find I'm nodding
in agreement at his humorous lament,
(a charitable view): *This book is plodding.*

A note: *Thereafter it's tragedy up to the end.*
A stretched-out phrase. I wonder where he sat
to write it. This chair? We who discommend
enact our allegory. And so, another caveat:
The book's so slow, John Keats at 21 feels 52.
I close the book and gaze towards the view.

Going Home

As the port grows larger
in the porthole,
I think I know what I'd prefer
my landfall to be:

A sweet island.
A language that hasn't changed.
A citizenly arrival.
Somebody I used to know—

the fabulous
bird-woman, whose telephone number
I lost, will come pecking her way
to greet me.

What plumage!
What a landscape! How deep! How soft!
What handsome trains waiting to leave
for the mountains! What mystical currency!

And there the reception committee will be—
all of it—smiling at me.
Accepting the welcoming gift
of a huge egg, I will be home.

Two for Nerval

FANTASY

There's a melody for which I'd give
All Mozart, Weber, all Rossini;
An ancient air. It languishes. Is dreamy.
For me alone its charming secrets live.

Each time I come into its hearing,
Two hundred years flow back. My soul is young.
A vanished time, through which I see appearing
A green hill, burnished from the setting sun.

Then a chateau, brick and edged in stone,
With leaded windows tinged a subtle red,
Surrounded by a park, a river flowing
Through banks of flowers, about the castlehead.

A woman high up at a window leans
Toward me. Fair or dark? I gaze enthralled.
From a previous life I know her, so it seems . . .
And feel it surge . . . the rush of my recall!

Epitaph

Blithely he lived, as only a flute can tell,
By turns amorous, carefree and tender,
Though sometimes dream-dark as a sad Clitander.
One day at his door, a person rang the bell.

It was Death. Asking him to wait,
He placed the full stop to his final sonnet
And then, without undue excitement, laid
His quivering form within the clammy casket.

He was lazy. So history will testify.
At his desk he let the ink run dry.
He experienced nothing, yet wanted to know.

Fatigued with life, at last the moment came.
One winter evening, his soul was wrenched away.
He went, enquiring: "Did I come, only to go?"

Magyarország

(1) Cukrászda

Nobody would thank me
    for *my* opinion
        the wind says,
but Hungary remains
    blowdown flat
        a low topography
though mostly contradicted by
    the hats on heads
        of gossipy ladies:
brim-crisp bowlers,
    green hunters,
        wound-about cloches.
This is a country
    where people seem O
        irritated.
Wouldn't *you* be irritated
    in your baroque salon
        by sweet stiflement?
Cakes, coffee, iced water,
    conversation which never
        endangers.
Nobody would thank me
    for shooting my
        old Jäger hat off,
rising to shatter
    the mirrors and cutlery,
        waiters diving for cover.
If my eyes were to fracture
    with tears or death
        who would finish my coffee?
But Hungary persists

               and suppose there is hope
                      you can't smell?
           Hmmm. Of coffee. Old ladies
                   with fantastic hats,
                        who've known
           Magyar twists of the arm,
                      loss of menfolk,
                         birds flying off,
           drink in the vaulted room,
                       the hush of water,
                           sweet continuance.

(II) Aruház

What's for sale? You have
           (bitterly) money,
               you have that
which you seem to look for.
           Is that money?
               I'm old
and my shoulders' landslip
           creeps to part
                my body from pride,
an old coat covering it up,
           and my spectacles,
                the great fissure.
I can't see without being told
           what to see. This
                is a queue.
First a queue to choose and then
           a queue to pay and then
                a queue to wrap—

[112]

                three queues for plastic shoes!
                        It's so hot in here,
                                I feel defeat,
                a kind of sickness
                            (bitterly) to choose
                                    between the things
                you know you may
                            and feel the past
                                    say loud and clear: "Do not!"

(III) Villamos

Yellow trams I've liked
            always the rumble
                    and clanking,
the unimpeded steel glide
            that parts the traffic
                    and the clink of the bell.
Thread of rackety iron
            the city is sewn
                    up tight by you.
Inside we do not speak
            as we grate and jolt
                    over the bridge,
the Elizabeth bridge, and look
            through the window at
                    the river's curve,
where St Matyas church stands
            up on the hill, and the river
                    ignores us,
downcast, silent, feeling
            iron wheels beneath,

        grinding but holding on;
where one white cloud fills
      the unmoved sky
          and we run along
the Danube's edge,
    gazing across
        while nothing changes,
as the yellow trams clatter and bang
      through old streets
          filled with silence.

(IV) POLITIKA

Politics is what you do
        to people you don't like.
           It may be
That things are best left
      as the piano-player is
          playing beautifully somewhere
in a long Hungarian afternoon,
      seeming to be there or here,
        but far off,
not really attended to.
      I think most things
         may be like this
and cross to be nearer.
      Mysteriously, the music goes
        further off.
The player stumbles
    on a note
        then tries again.
In a restaurant doorway

                a waiter listens:
                        Mozart not quite accurate,
wages and currency *never*
                        accurate, hope
beginning again. Who,
                as he climbs the street,
                        is immune?
And I think: "He is starting over"
                and cross back
                        to a park
where the old people rest and stare
                across the pigeons
                        at a tourist.
Most things seem to be like this:
                not political, except
                        in the soul.

(v) Magyarország

A pot of geraniums
                bright yellow against green
                        window-frames.
Wide earth and wide sky.
                An open petal of skiffs
                        by river-shore.
The fierce Magyar
                with horse and whip
                        seeds your mind:
A hero, risen
                from scalding chicken-broth
                        to call to his followers,
while the men listen,

[115]

    in the dark *étterem*,
      and the sky peters out.
Old burnt-mouth.
    A language of
      back-vowels.
If you must have a lesson
    the best lesson
      is a kind of picture:
Miles of sunflowers.
    Solar acquiescence.
      Daylong silence.
But when we speak
    knives between our teeth:
      back-vowels.

Glossary

Magyarország: the state of Hungary
Cukrászda: a coffee (and cake) shop
Aruház: department store
Villamos: tramway
Étterem: restaurant

Ode to a Paella
For Marta Pessarodonna

The rice is best, Marta, you're right,
this gluey, saffron-coloured, mouth-entrancing
mound of sea-infatuated stuff:
The sea was dancing. We glimpsed
it through the windows and the doors
to remind us of the world beyond
our dark flat pan of joy,
prawns and monster crayfish and mussel-shells,
the taste of colours: *rose* and black and *jaune*.
The wine was cold as sea in March.
Moodily we talked, the way a day has temper—
harmonic passages, problems left absurd.
And now, to each green-peppered, oceanic,
cosmically tender forkful, I raise my pen to write:
"Look, Marta, this is what I've found!"

Five Anecdotes of the Count

(1) NOBILITY

Chased from my remarkable sleep,
Observed the Count, I strode
To the tall window, a winter grey,
And looked down at the cobbles,
A bench, the sodden leaves of autumn.
I thought a carriage might have passed, but
Two naked trees proclaimed a silence.
Beyond them lay the town, a little smudged,
As though a child's thumb had rubbed
The pastels and the charcoal to confusion—
Clear line not visible. This place I lodged in
Seemed tense with women, serving men,
Waiting on my matinal enlightenment.
My hat and rapier were cold upon a stool.
A briefcase on the bed contained my poems.
Sitting at an easel I'd have liked
To sketch the countenance of someone,
No matter who, that they should be
Transformed within my ultra-sighted gaze.
The light just right.
The chimney breast, the walls, were throbbing.
I felt the heat contained within the wainscot—
Does a lion fear the creaking of the wheel?

Descending, half-attired, to the parlour,
I ate the ham and sausage placed before me
Within a vast, cold room, whose grate contained
The sour ashes of the night before. I think
The serving-people may have been,
Perhaps I'm wrong,
The spectral folk who populate my dreams—

Ingratiating, colourless. They crushed
Their hands in deference, their foreheads stooped.
With comical humility they left me, in reverse.
I wiped my mouth.

          On the doorstep, muddy air
Still ripe with rain, and fogged,
Cleansed off the beer from my throat.
A carriage, I recall,
Swerved from under the arch, then away.
Two faces glistened at the window:
Pale brides of destiny. I feel
Such salient encounters with spreading shock
As though my veins grew out beyond my skin.
I watched them clatter down the hill,
Aware of people from the inn
Watching me as I went splashing round the yard
Without a hat. Watching as I plucked
A final leaf from off the tree,
Shook water-drops upon my cheek.
Watching as I raised my knee and placed
A booted foot upon the wall
That overlooked a sheer embankment
And came to rest.

I stared across an infinite yet tiny space.
The veiled town below was like my thought:
In different shades, the light divulged
This plain reality we talk so much about
And never share. It pleased me
To be contemplating this, and to be
Contemplated in my turn—no one
Knowing how the crystals of my thought

Formed, re-formed, dissolved and changed
Within the cloudy vial of my brain.
What could they think of this?
I felt exhilaration shiver in my bones.
Never had I felt so pleased
Both with myself and with my acumen.
Remarked by all (their faces whitening
                            the window-panes,)
Unjacketed, and with a former sailor's grace,
I turned to look at them,
And I began to dance.

(2) SENSUALITY

Tired of my loves and furies,
The Count related, I took
The steam train up into the mountains,
Plucking grasses from the rocky wall
By hand, so slowly up the gradient
We went. A peasant woman with
A sullen face groped for my regard.
Her figure was good. I felt
The feral air of Spring
Enclose my heart's reluctant
Mildness. Then
We clanked unkindly to a standstill,
Lurched and blew out hoots and vapour.
She walked off through the crowd
Yet turned back once or twice to meet
My eyes. It makes me shudder still.
To think of that intensity

Each day I walked beside the lake
To watch the fish be caught.
The gravel clicked and roared
Beneath my feet, each
Silent-standing tree absolved the light.
After sunset I would try to study
Classics, cracked and stained,
Unreadable. My body
Seemed to resonate and thrum
In some place echoing
Against a wall of darkness.
When morning came
I always seemed to meet
Young women from the farm—
Curtseying, their smiles like milk—
Or serving-girls who left the path,
Scurried to the trees and waited there
Till I had passed. They
Watched me go: I heard their breath:
O all manner of infantile things!
But I was quite without desire.
Innocence is the resort of the dull.
I longed for a superb mockery—
A counterfeit eagle to sweep from hell!

Taking a book of verse for the form's sake,
I stopped by the big kitchen
Enquiring after scones.
I placed them wrapped into my musette
And went off, hopefully, towards the mountain.
The ground rose steeply to a track
And by a pile of fresh-cut wood:
The peasant woman.

She smiled. I recognised the one
For whom a better word perhaps is
Precognition. I fell into the stupor
Of her gaze. Stopped dead.
Someone you must one day meet, there is,
Who knows just what you are,
Who lives the gravid line
That leads away from doubt, and seems
To nourish, limitless, a craving you
Could not, till then, materialise.
Her figure was good. Un-
Buttoning her lace chemise, un-
Hooking straps that slung across
A pure white shoulder,
She leaned herself against the wood,
Arched and darkly soft like some reproach
Of memory for acts that I
In prowling youth had best left not
Performed.
             The Count broke off. Resumed.
What's best left not related is
The truth. I went on past, and yet
I had to look back once. Or was it, maybe, twice?
The path ran down beside the tump of logs
And nothing moved there—empty
Greenery, as if to say
Imagination, Count, imagination.
D'you know that song, French I think it is:
In the centre of the bed
The river there is deep?
Well, there are those
The current sweeps away,
An arm raised from the spray, from

The swirling debris. My vision
Falters before darkness, before whiteness.
I continued a long way up that hill.
Neither up nor down, you
Might say, I squatted on a rock
Thinking of someone in whom
Desire and love had come so boundlessly together
It had to break. And
The etched peak of the mountain remained—
Patterns from a distance—
I am no climber.
I could see the snowfield near the top,
Where no one had walked, but where
Irresistibly, my mind led me.
Taking my pipe out, I fingered in tobacco,
Lit it, knowing
Deep, intrinsic loneliness
The fragrant veils of smoke obscured,
Under the dwarfing elbow of the mountain,
By the heights of an inland sea.

(3) BUSINESS

I knew the Bailiff had invented her.
Remarked the Count, a flight
To an outlying farm, her simplicity.
His face came close to mine
To share the male thing he thought
We had in common: *If I could give
Some help, you understand?* And he:
Implicit in my good discretion,
Who'd never miss a chance to tell

A better story. So was he really
What he said the women said he was?
I guessed he'd found another stratagem
To profit from my vain compassion.

Many were waiting for an interview,
Loafing in the corridor outside,
But Gabriel had sent me proofs.
I could not help imagining his shop,
The browsers leafing through the stock.
Would they murder for the latest verse?
They'd cut, at any rate, the pages
To find out how the metre
Was resolved. You don't believe me?
Quite right.
Quite right.

And if I knew that she did not exist
Why did I believe him?
I have often retreated to another room
When guests arrived I could not face,
Knowing that man was always somewhere
Holding civil conversation—brutally civil!
I gazed upon his britches.
Six children had spurted
From that piece of flesh
The stained leather concealed. At
Cheating-tide would he confess all? The books
Were cooked again, he knew I knew
He knew I could afford it. Would I come then
To Dreadful Grief, that they used to say about me?
(Voice no doubts to women.)
I could not swear

That the smell of woodsmoke in March
Was not more beautiful to me
Than poetry.

    Bring them in,
I said. My workmen
Showed me deference from puzzlement.
The Bailiff flattered them with his authority.
I hemmed and hawed at thatches, planting out—
They were unreal, shadowy,
Till one said: "You ate garlic for breakfast,
Sir. You stink as sweetly to me
As my wife does at bedtime,
For she loves spring garlic. And then
When she is naked and smells like that
I am a rat, Sir,
Or a rumbling stone. At least
I am not myself."
I stared, then questioned him,
And I won't swear he smiled.
He said: "The answer must be 'Yes,
Sir,' though I came
About another matter."

I made him Bailiff straightaway
And sacked the confidential fellow
On the spot. It isn't possible
To first approve and then advance a man
Unless, like me,
You're worthless and in power.

(4) Personal Effects

(1)

I do not affect unkemptness,
The Count said, it comes to me
Naturally, like mischief.
A stained heart, a filthy chemise,
One verifies the other.
Brooding on the walls of my house
Where I sit at my desk in candle-light,
Not even a dog moves.
But there is a beast in this labyrinth
Growling at my bafflement,
My unlaced boots,
The *déshabille* of my thoughts.
In the cave of language it is dark.
I listen to myself
As one who holds a torch against the wall
To see what's scribbled there.
Round the fire, outside, a hubbub
Swoops around owl-heavy trees.
Bound by a spell of contemplation
I trace the curve of a word,
Working it gently from the mud of mind.
The power of the word is now
To the power of nothing, except
To the power of a hammer on a skull.
Will they burst in on me with torches
Trying to light what's
Lit already, beyond mere seeing?

(11)

My poems are in print now,
As Gabriel reports. The browsers' dirty
Hands are at them; what
Is that but vanity to offer up such things?
And then immediately wounding is
The thought of subtle smiles upon
The reader's faces. Here, in the evening,
I sit and re-walk that lost country
That made me write, wearing my memory
Down at heel as I climb the hill, higher and higher,
Absorbed with the village below me—
Rapt in its forgetfulness-of-soul.
Rooftops, chimneys, windows—they move
Me inexplicably, yet the blankness
Of my house-walls go on darkening
And gather to a tryst, the ultimate
Unremembering. Upwards, my friend.
The greened wood of a rotting gate
Swells open, brushing the dew from grass-tops.
I go through where old tracks
Have not been used awhile. The ground
Rises, sloping, like my mind,
Thoughts I cannot see over—
Did I tell you, mused the Count,
That something yonder is turning to stare at me?

(5) ABROAD

Travel sweetens the soul,
The Count reflected, it is the space
Between doubt. I looked down once

Upon the face of a girl I had slept with,
Previously, previously. A face
Which had looked at other things,
Which had used other words,
Which had gone inevitably forward.
We had been away so long all doubt
Dissolved. Yet I forget now
If she smiled back, or even
Pretended to remember. There is no security
In the past.
                Another time
I was invited to a foreign city,
Not knowing the language, a land of squabble
Or love, it was hard to tell
Which was which. I saw a drunk
Tossed from a doorway. I saw a dog
Accost a bone. Such memories I keep
Carefully, as the rooms of my house,
At home, are carefully swept by others.
I buckled on my sword and walked the streets
To the tavern we had spoken of—
That area of wine and laughter
Which lies between the poles
Of dank necessity. Those foreign poets!
A recitation was in progress—
Verse in a tongue I could not follow.
I accepted the challenge and the wine,
Told them the story of my life
In disrelated vocables, noises
Of artful lips and teeth, clicks
Of the palate—surprised to find my passion there,
From a great conflagration
To a trickle of water-drops!

                            The Count smiled:
It brought the house down.
I said we should sing and drink to freedom;
I believe they were amused.
We clapped for the gypsies to approach:
The fiddler's cat-gut pined at my ear.
I thrust a new bank-note
Under the bridge of his violin. From
Far off I could hear something else;
There was water moving in my soul.
I wear, as you see, expensive clothes without
Precaution, considered by most
A presentable man. But leaky.
                            I am dripping away
Into the garrulous universe.
What is not fierce of focus in me
The muttering darkness out there
Appears to crave. Always, always
Too excitable, I took
A partner, dancing frantically,
But found myself, much later, by the river,
Quite alone. I looked across
At inns and dancing places on the other bank—
A string of incandescent invitations—
I was listening to another recitation,
A fresh poem that splashed through my head
Like rain through the roof.
A question:
            Is the structure of this,
A poem, is the fabric of it
Merely to threaten and tear away,
Becoming at last what I had
Already wished to be without knowing it?

You could imagine the fearfulness
Of my presentiments. And an old man
Suddenly spoke to me in that weird dialect,
And I understood:
"New stars, right treaties, let the spaces live!"

Moment Abbey

Did you hear the bell ring
in Moment Abbey, children?
Climbing did you quickly pluck
yourselves from shaky branches
and lie windfall listening
to the organ's stern harangue?

Do you hear your teeth
in apples, children?
Biting will you bite again
and fill your heads with noise
of carols, sound of choristers
in surplices of time?

Will you chase the music
In Abbey orchard, children?
Playing touch, will screams of laughter
fill your head with ancient sound.
And when you stop and turn
will you be 'It' and be alone?

Walking can you hear the children
laughing in the empty orchard?
Standing, can you see the spire
where once it stood?
And listen! Can you hear the bells
so silent, apple-like and true?

Pan's Joke

The furious and mortal pipes of love
were playing in the valley of regret;
I heard them from my scullery of art,
where dishes, children, music, filled the sink.

A band of brass began to belch and grunt,
the townsfolk hauled aloft the flag of hope;
I wandered out beyond the limits of resolve,
and climbed foolhardy hill without a thought.

The tune was like a beast of indecision.
I heard it as I walked among the breeze.
I gathered armfuls of her hair
I gathered what my senses could not spare.

The road, the farmhouse and the river,
like brilliant flaws within the warp of time,
responded in their glittering to her:
three silver prophesies upon the plain.

I made the mould of air contain myself.
I made it print me, duplicate.
I had it wrapped around my shape.
I populated all this range of hills.

And she? O she is sleeping, music-
girl whose melody this is.
Her eyes that opened for a kiss have closed,
her lover's breath no more upon her face.

While I gesticulate and wave, a frieze
of dancing scarecrows, absurd atop
each cairn. O music leave me! No! Return!
You furious and mortal pipes of love.